Dear ______________________ ______,
On your birth and Baptism, wishing you
____
____
With love from ______________
Date ______________

Translated from the original entitled:
Mein schönes Fest der Taufe.
Erinnerungsalbum

by Ulrike Graumann
Illustrations by Bernadette Nagel

English translation by *Anne Marie Swift*

Middle Green
Slough SL3 6BS
www.pauline-uk.org e-mail: productions@pauline-uk.org

Printed by
SIG - Soc. Industrial Gráfica, Lda. - Camarate (Portugal)
Printed March 2002
First reprint June 2002
ISBN 0 9538540 2 7

Celebrating My Baptism

Illustrations by Bernadette Nagel

Pauline
BOOKS & MEDIA

All about me:

My name is ______________________________

I was born on ______________ at ________ am/pm

in ______________________________________

I weighed ________ at birth, and measured ________ long.

My head measured ______________

I love my mother and father.

Their names are __________________

My first photograph

Grandmother
Grandfather
Father
My family tree
Brother
Me

In every apple there is space for the name and a little photo of each member of your family. If there are not enough apples draw some more on coloured card and stick them on this page.

This is me before I was born:
(a photo of my mother
when she was expecting me
or of a scan)

My parents knew on ______________________

that I was on the way and was growing inside my mother.

They thought of lots of names for me:

____

if I was a boy, and

____

if I was a girl.

The doctors calculated that I would arrive on ______________________

And I was actually born on

____

I stayed in hospital for ______ days.

My first days in hospital were like this:

____

____

I was helped into this world by

the obstetrician ______________________________

the midwife / the doctor ________________________

My first toys and presents were:

These are the people who came to see me in hospital:

When they saw me they said things like:

These are some of the messages of congratulations we received:

What was happening on the day I was born

in my home town

in my country

in the world

Here is a cutting from a newspaper
on the day I was born.

On ______________ I came home

to ___________________________

____

It looks like this:

These are the members of my family:

This is my birth certificate.

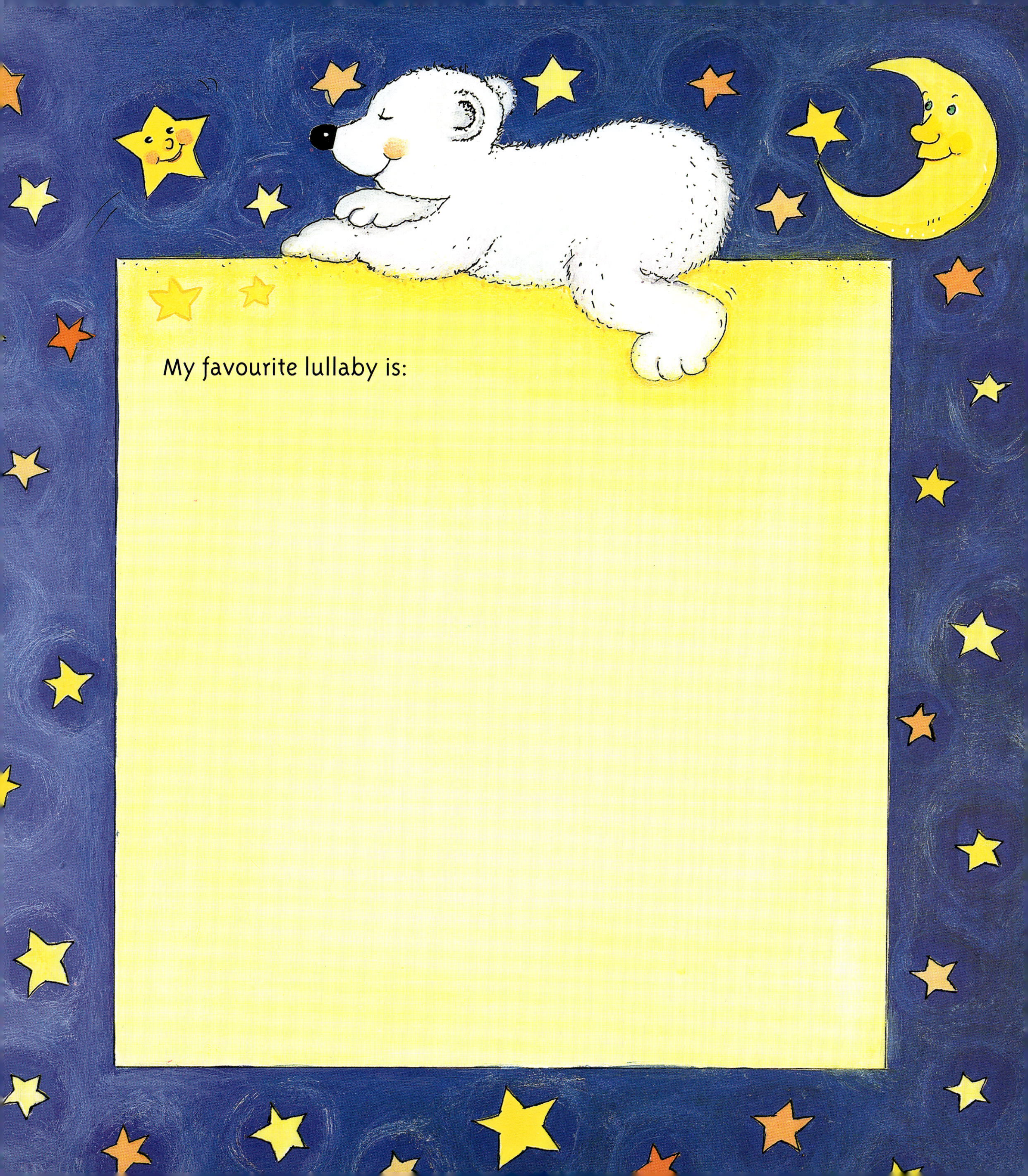

My favourite lullaby is:

We celebrated my Baptism

on ________________________________

I received the sacrament of Baptism

in the Church of ________________________________

in ________________________________

at __________ am/pm

The priest or deacon who baptised me is called

____

My parents and godparents were with me on this special day.

My godmother's name is ______________________________

and I call her ______________________________

My godfather's name is ______________________________

and I call him ______________________________

With us at my Baptism were:

____

____

____

This is a photo of my Baptism
and some of the cards I received.

My Baptism is a real celebration.

To start with, the priest/deacon asks my parents:
"What name do you give your child?"

My parents reply " ______________________ "

"What do you ask of God's Church for __________ ?"
"**Baptism"** they answer.

The priest or deacon then says:
"Dear parents, you have asked to have your child baptised. In doing so you are accepting the responsibility of training him/her in the practice of the faith. It will be your duty to bring him/her up to keep God's commandments as Christ taught us, by loving God and our neighbour. Do you clearly understand what you are undertaking?"
My parents answer: **"We do"**.

Then the priest/deacon speaks
to my godmother and godfather:
**"Are you prepared to help the parents
in their duty as Christian parents?"**
And my godparents reply: **"We are".**

The priest/deacon then speaks to me.

" ______________________________
**the Christian community welcomes you with great joy.
In its name, I claim you for Christ our Saviour
by the sign of his cross.
I now trace the cross on your forehead,
and invite your parents (and godparents) to do the same".**

The SIGN OF THE CROSS
is the first of a series of small actions
which all have great significance.

We listen to these readings:

____

____

____

We pray to the saints, including the saint whose name I share.

Then the priest/deacon anoints me on the chest
with the OIL of catechumens, saying:
"We anoint you with the oil of salvation
in the name of Christ our Saviour;
may he strengthen you with his power,
who lives and reigns for ever and ever".

A long time ago sportsmen used to be
anointed with oil before starting a race.
I too want to train so that the love of Jesus will triumph.

The Baptism continues with the blessing of the WATER.
Water is a sign of life. In fact, it is the fount of life
because nothing can grow without it. And we wash ourselves with water.
So water is a sign of purification. It purifies the body and the soul.

The word Baptism means "immersion".
The priest/deacon will immerse me three times in the water
or pour a little of the water over my head.

First, the water is blessed.
Then all those present declare their faith in God,
replying **"I do"** to three questions put by the priest/deacon.
And now, the moment of the actual Baptism arrives.

The priest/deacon asks my parents and godparents:

"Is it your will that ____________________
should be baptised in the faith of the Church,
which we have all professed with you?"
My parents and godparents answer: **"It is".**
The priest/deacon then baptises me,
wetting my head three times with water, while saying:

" ____________________, I baptise you
in the name of the Father,
and of the Son,
and of the Holy Spirit".

The priest or deacon makes a sign on my head
with CHRISM, a special oil blended with perfume,
which has been blessed by the bishop.
The kings and prophets of the people of Israel
were consecrated with this kind of perfumed oil.
Like them, and like Jesus, I too am called
to do something great and important.

The priest/deacon gives me
a WHITE GARMENT, saying:
“ ______________ **, you have become a new creation**
and have clothed yourself in Christ.
See in this white garment
the outward sign of your Christian dignity.
With your family and friends
to help you by word and example,
bring that dignity unstained into
the everlasting life of heaven”.

Then my parents and godparents light
a CANDLE from the big Easter candle on the altar.
"Receive the light of Christ", says the priest or deacon.
"Parents and godparents,
this light is entrusted to you
to be kept burning brightly.
This child of yours has been
enlightened by Christ.
He/she is to walk always as a child of the light.
May he/she keep the flame
of faith alive in his/her heart.
When the Lord comes,
may he/she go out to meet him
with all the saints in the heavenly kingdom".

At this point, the priest /deacon
may perform the EPHPHETHA.
Like Jesus in the Gospel, the priest/deacon touches
my ears and mouth with his thumb, saying:
"The Lord Jesus made the deaf hear and the dumb speak.
May he soon touch your ears to receive his word,
and your mouth to proclaim his faith,
to the praise and glory of God the Father".

We then all pray the OUR FATHER:

Our Father,
who art in heaven,
hallowed be thy name;
thy kingdom come;
thy will be done on earth
as it is in heaven.
Give us this day our daily bread
and forgive us our trespasses
as we forgive those
who trespass against us;
and lead us not into temptation,
but deliver us from evil.

At the end, the priest/deacon pronounces
a BLESSING for my mother,
one for my father, and another for all those present.
A blessing for me
and other children being baptised is:
**"May God the almighty Father,
who filled the world with joy
by giving us his only Son,
bless this newly-baptised child.
May he/she grow
to be more fully like
Jesus Christ, our Lord."**

The celebration of my Baptism continued.

We went to:

And we celebrated by:

Here are the names
of everyone
who was invited.
They can sign
with a message too.

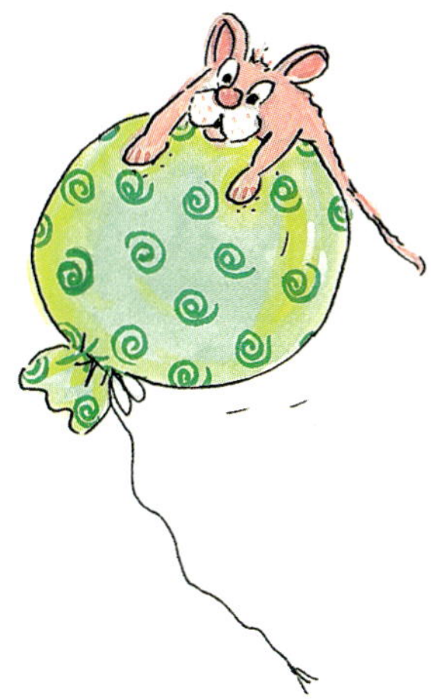

Photographs of my celebration.

My name and my patron saint's name is:

My patron saint's feast day is on:

____

This is what I know about my patron saint:

This is what my parents pray for me:

Loving God and Father

we thank you for giving us ______________________

who brings us great joy

and who brings us closer to you.

May we always remain in your love

throughout life's journey. Amen.

Most evenings, my parents pray for me like this:

____

____

____

____

____

____

MAKING PROGRESS!

I know how to:

What I like best is:

I don't like:

My first movements were:

My first words were:

I said "mummy" for the first time on:

I said "daddy" for the first time on:

I ate my first baby food on: